CANDLES IN THE CITY

CANDLES IN THE CITY

G. CURTIS JONES

WORD BOOKS, Publisher
Waco, Texas

CANDLES IN THE CITY BY G. CURTIS JONES

Library of Congress catalog card number: 72–96356
Printed in the United States of America

TO

THE CITY CHURCHES
I HAVE SERVED AS SENIOR MINISTER

Seventh Street Christian Church
Richmond, Virginia

Vine Street Christian Church
Nashville, Tennessee

Union Avenue Christian Church
St. Louis, Missouri

University Christian Church
Des Moines, Iowa

and

Woodland Christian Church
Macon, Georgia

WITH GRATITUDE AND LOVE

CONTENTS

Introduction 11

1. ON REMEMBERING YOUR FIRST LOVE 15
2. ON BEING FAITHFUL 25
3. ON BEING TOO TOLERANT 37
4. ON HOLDING FAST 47
5. ON STAYING ALIVE 55
6. ON BEING OBEDIENT 67
7. ON BEING ENTHUSIASTIC 79

The Scene 89

ACKNOWLEDGMENTS

Writing a book is a corporate accomplishment. It is an intertwining of skill and spirit, aspiration and commitment, excitement and hard work.

I would like to thank all who assisted in producing *Candles in the City*. Gratitude is expressed to a number of perceptive readers. Among them: George S. Pease, former Editor of Publications, Equitable of Iowa, Sun City Center, Florida; Marvin G. Osborn, Jr., Financial Consultant, St. Louis, Missouri; James S. Duncan, School of Journalism, and John E. McCaw, Department of Philosophy and Religion, Drake University, Des Moines, Iowa; Douglas S. Looney, Better Homes and Gardens, Des Moines; and our son, Paul Jones, Yale University, New Haven, Connecticut. As with all aspects of my ministry, Sybil's patient understanding through the gestation period of this book is also appreciated.

I am particularly indebted to my secretary, Mrs. Charles L. Patrick, for meticulous care in researching and preparing the manuscript.

G. Curtis Jones

INTRODUCTION

It is better to light one candle than to curse the darkness.
The Christophers

Candles in the City recalls the fascinating and disturbing problems of ancient city churches as described in Revelation and relates them to life in the contemporary urban setting. Proclamation of the gospel began in the city, not in the country.

Banished to the lonely Aegean island of Patmos because of his Christian faith, John, author of the Bible's most dramatic and apocalyptic book, Revelation, declared he was visited by an angel bearing witness to the Word of God. Receiving the ethereal message, he then prophetically and courageously addressed the seven persecuted urban congregations in Asia Minor.

Because of the mysterious nature of John's vision with which our Bible concludes, its eschatological coloring, imagery, symbols, and idioms, the tendency has been to neglect, if not wholly miss, its unique and continuing relevancy. To me it is a point of immense significance that early Christians promptly penetrated powerful and arrogant cities with the gospel of Christ.

Aware of conditions and pending judgments, John saluted the congregations of Asia Minor: "Grace to you and peace from him who is and who was and who is to come, and from the seven spirits who are before his throne, and from Jesus Christ the faithful witness, the first-born of the dead, and the ruler of kings on earth" (Rev. 1:4–5, RSV).

Identifying himself as John, their brother in Christ, he declared, "I was in the Spirit on the Lord's day" (Rev. 1:10, RSV). John heard a voice like a trumpet. Turning in the direction of "the voice," he beheld "seven golden lampstands" in the midst of which stood one who resembled a "son of man," dressed in flowing robes, girded with a golden belt, and with hair white as snow. His eyes flashed like fire; his feet were as bright as polished brass; his voice was that of a waterfall. In his right hand were seven stars. A two-edged sword protruded from his mouth, while his face shone with the brilliance of the sun. Frightened, the seer fell at the feet of the Presence who told him the seven lampstands were the churches. Being assured, he was admonished to write.

Like the One whom he served amid overpowering evil, Roman regimentation and control, John had not given up on God nor become an alumnus of the Church. The story of man's liberation in Christ was all-consuming. He believed light had come into the world and nothing could extinguish it. Like a lamp not hidden but exhibited, he believed the Church of Jesus Christ would reflect luminous love, unquenchable light, and would ultimately penetrate and save evil cities from their sins.

The King James Version of Scripture renders the phrase *seven golden lampstands* to read "seven golden candlesticks." We seldom see a lamp except in antique shops, but candles are common and generally associated with celebrations.

Knowledge and experience prevent one from referring to the Church as the brilliant and irresistible light of Christ in the city. It is not. Physically its glow is scarcely discernible amid the glaring neon lights of Broadway, the psychedelic lights of night spots, the beckoning lights of business, and the massive floodlights of sporting arenas. However gaudy or mammoth, if there is a shortage of voltage due to overload, disaster, or malfunction, electric lights go out. Candles, less complicated, more exposed, more beautiful because they consume themselves while providing light for others, are more dependable.

The city has always attracted man. It symbolizes his sophistication and hides his sin. Throughout history a differentiation has been made between the city of man and the City of God. However, the Gospels and John's Revelation emphasize more than man's migration to metropolises. They challenge him—through the initiative of forgiveness and love—to reshape and redeem his community.

New Jerusalem, the new city, is not only where injustices are abolished; inequities corrected; the lost found; sick attended; poor rehabilitated; the hungry fed; the exploited liberated; but also the scene of joy and celebration because the light of Christ dispels the darkness and fears from the streets.

Despite criticism of the Church, I like to think of it as God's candle in the city; not yet a beacon, a tall taper. At times its light is infinitesimal. Caretakers permit it to burn low, even out. But only for a brief time! Some soul living in prison, ghetto, hospital, outer space, kitchen, office, or study, viewing the ancient cross, lights his candle again and turns homeward with hope.

1

On Remembering Your First Love

CONTRARY TO THE EARLY AMERICAN PATTERN OF ESTABLISHing rural churches, early Christians penetrated cities with the Good News of Christ. The Book of Revelation, full of cryptic symbols, idioms, and figures of ancient speech, nevertheless communicates the unveiling of the Church by Christ and the dimensions of the Christian community in frightening and dramatic terms.

John, the voice in this remarkable book, saw the Church symbolized by seven golden candlesticks, the perfect number, flickering in the night like tapers in a breeze. Living with memories and hopes on the island of Patmos, John's moving vision of the constellation of churches began with Ephesus.

Perhaps Ephesus could be referred to as the Boston or New York City of the Mediterranean world, founded a thousand years before Christ. It was noted for its culture, theaters, architecture, and was the home of the temple of Diana. Such stalwarts as Paul, Timothy, Priscilla, and

Aquila could identify with the people of Ephesus. Imagine that handful of heterogeneous believers in indiscriminate dress attempting to penetrate such an establishment! Yet this is precisely what they undertook and accomplished.

John congratulated the hearty disciples on their endurance, faithfulness, and suffering. Going beyond their obvious accomplishments, however, he said: "I have this against you, that you have abandoned the love you had at first. Remember then from what you have fallen, repent and do the works you did at first. If not, I will come to you and remove your lampstand from its place, unless you repent" (Rev. 2:4–5, RSV).

If John's indictment seems harsh to a crusading people centuries ago, how much more pertinent and disturbing are his words when applied to affluent America? Have professing Christians traded conviction for culture; evangelism for efficiency; compassion for computers?

The modern city not only generates and controls wealth, creates standards and styles, but also is the home of hope, for it is where the majority of people live. Prior to 1900 more than half of our citizens lived in the country; now 75 percent live in urban centers. Present trends are toward "strip cities" such as Philadelphia-New York-Boston, Washington-Baltimore, Jacksonville-Miami, Milwaukee-Chicago, and Dallas-Fort Worth. It is predicted that four-fifths of our population will live in such megalopolises by 1980.

In this concrete wilderness surfeited with crime, violence, congestion, misery, and sin, the Church is commissioned to minister. At a time when cities are quivering with emphysema of their own creation, the Church is challenged to open spiritual windows that the prevailing winds of God might refresh and redeem mankind.

How is one to know and share love in such a polluted and hostile environment? How is this ancient, rurally oriented and nurtured gospel, born in heaven though fleshed in Palestine, to find respect and acceptance in a highly complex world? How can a Roman cross exposing a crucified Jew to sun, gnats, and flies, possibly communicate God's love to a sophisticated, technological society? What place has the continuing good news of God's love in computerized America?

It is in this fermenting, frightening, heckling, bankrupt, unsafe, noisy, dirty city that Jesus would have his disciples be the Church!

"You have abandoned the love you had at first." These words are as relevant and haunting as if they had been uttered from the Astrodome in Houston, or from a spaceship, congratulating America on her accomplishments but vigorously condemning her sins.

Do you remember your first love? The first time you saw your mother's face, recognized your father's strength, realized the solidarity and supportiveness of your family? Do you remember, with the developing years, your increased responsibilities, chores, schedules? Your pet? I shall never forget my first horse nor the acre of tobacco which was mine to cultivate.

Have you forgotten that first date, the high-school prom . . . your first love? Remember the courtship and marriage of Elizabeth Barrett and Robert Browning? Robert persuaded Elizabeth to leave her invalid's couch and elope with him. In the sunny warmth of Italy she regained strength. During this time she wrote—not for publication but for her husband—enchanting words wherein she declared that she had loved him from the first time she heard the footsteps of his soul.

> How do I love thee? Let me count the ways.
> I love thee to the depth and breadth and height
> My soul can reach, when feeling out of sight
> For the ends of Being and ideal Grace.
> I love thee to the level of every day's
> Most quiet need, by sun and candle-light.
> I love thee freely, as men strive for Right;
> I love thee purely, as they turn from praise.
> I love thee with the passion put to use
> In my old griefs, and with my childhood's faith.
> I love thee with a love I seemed to lose
> With my lost saints,—I love thee with the breath,
> Smiles, tears, of all my life!—and, if God choose,
> I shall but love thee better after death.

First loves can also be painful memories, experiences that redirect and reshape life. I am thinking of a former parishioner, physician, who, disappointed in love, never married. Instead he made a home for unfortunate boys and sent dozens of young men through high school and college. When I asked how many he had assisted, his answer was a soft rebuke, "I never count them."

A first love haunts many for life. Despite debate surrounding the love of Ann Rutledge and Abraham Lincoln, following her death Abe walked the brink of insanity.

When Elly Lou Axon died, a bereft Woodrow Wilson wrote, "God has stricken me almost beyond what I can bear." She was fifty. They had been married twenty-nine years, but by his own admission he had loved her since childhood. Standing at a White House window overlooking the garden she had planted, the president prayed again and again, "O my God, what am I going to do? What am I going to do?"

Consider Alan Paton's intimate and tender story *For You Departed: A Memoir*. In a reflective, conversational style the poet-reformer of South Africa shares the exhilarating experience when first he met Dorrie. With great dignity and honesty he recalls their courtship, marriage, life together, grief at the knowledge of her pending death, and finally her homegoing in 1967. "Part of my longing," he writes, "is for myself, for my youth, for the days of my first love. . . ."

There is something precious about first loves.

Life has a way of crushing love. And no place is better equipped for this cruel business than the teeming city. Yet many of us enjoy the competition, challenge, and charm of the throbbing metropolis.

In the ever-increasing migration to urban centers, how is one to survive political ambush, economic disaster, temptations of marketplace and night spots? In a day when men walk more confidently among craters of the moon than through city parks, how is one to carry the candle of light and love through dangerous streets?

Ralph Barton was a popular cartoonist for *The New Yorker*. He is reported to have committed suicide, leaving behind this well-known and revealing confession: "I have had few real difficulties. I have had, on the contrary, an exceptionally glamorous life, as life goes, and I have had more than my share of affection and appreciation. The most charming, intelligent, and important people that I have known have liked me. . . . I have run from wife to wife, from house to house, and from country to country in a ridiculous effort to escape myself. . . . No one thing is responsible for this [suicide] and no person except myself. . . . I did it because I am fed up with inventing devices for getting through twenty-four hours a day."

The city, with all its allure, nonetheless has a way of running one ragged—distorting values, warping personality, freezing faith, and demythologizing humanity.

Dr. E. Stanley Jones tells of a girl who, frustrated by

the city, entered a house of prostitution. Learning of her daughter's plight, the mother desperately sought to rescue her. Not having her child's address, she left a photograph of herself in each house of ill-fame visited. One day the errant girl saw on a mantel in a reception room a familiar picture. It was the likeness of her first love—mother. Beneath were the words *come home*.

Do you remember your first encounter with Christ? Do you remember the circumstances that led to your belief in Christ as the Son of God? Do you remember your baptism, what your pastor said and your response? Do you remember how vibrant was your faith, or has the city chilled your Christian ardor? Has schedule smothered your spirit?

It is astonishing how easily Christian commitments are forgotten, especially when one moves to a metropolis. It is equally frustrating to encounter a spate of excuses why enthusiasm wanes and other interests take precedence over the Church. It requires more courage, more energy, a greater degree of total stewardship to bear witness for Christ in the city.

How well I recall our country church and the dear man who served as pastor for thirty years. He baptized me along with several other boys in a spring branch. I walked through a cornfield to a farmer's barn to change clothes. I can remember every detail of that day and the difference it made in my life, even though I have spent the majority of my years in urban settings. An abiding first love.

Do you remember how first you loved the Church? How proud you were to be a member? How kind you were to people? How you volunteered for service? Shortly after World War II a pastor in Frankfurt, Germany, told me he had one hundred men who would perform any ministry needed on brief notice. What a staff!

Many of us felt this way about the Church at first but we lost something of that love in the press of the city, in search of family security, in pursuit of personal success.

The Church is under attack. It always has been. Resentment to general conditions, institutionalism, especially as experienced in crowded megalopolises, has encouraged, if not increased, what Helmut Thielicke calls "existential illness." The rebellious individual is struggling to identify with purpose and power, to experience meaning and freedom. Secularism of the Church is so similar to that of the city that the man in the street cannot be sure if the Church is voice or echo, community or establishment.

On the theological left are intellectuals who say the only way for the Christian community to be relevant is to break with the past and create new forms of expression and ministry. Some would characterize themselves even more radically by saying the visible church should be destroyed. I sat through a terrible meeting. Participants were angry. A black man said, "Reconciliation between races can only be accomplished when white churches are burned to the ground . . . and their money given to the poor."

On the theological right are those who maintain the way out of our dilemma and doubt is a radical return to fundamentalism. Naturally these positions are incompatible. Perhaps we need to recapture the refrain of the prophet and envision the "righteous remnant," identify with the faithful, demonstrate the theology of hope, become a people ready to serve. With all her faults and inconsistencies, no other institution has taken the risks and is paying the price of love as is the Church.

Jesus wept over Jerusalem. He loved that city. Part of his sorrow emanated from the fact that Jerusalem possessed no theology of change. Although the so-called holy city epitomized magnificence, it did not recognize nor was it ready to receive the new, transforming spirit of love.

The Lord continues to weep over Jerusalem, London, Paris, Chicago, your city and mine. The ancient voice addressed to Ephesus comes to the American church with increasing clarity: "I know all about you: how hard you work and how much you put up with. I know you cannot stand wicked men, and how you tested the impostors who called themselves apostles and proved they were liars. I know, too, that you have patience, and have suffered for my name without growing tired. Nevertheless, I have this complaint to make; you have less love now than you used to" (Rev. 2:2–5, JB). What an obvious and inescapable condemnation!

Do you remember how eagerly you once defended your faith? Sometimes out of ignorance, sometimes out of intelligence or experience, but confident of your commitment you stood up to be counted at the slightest threat to your belief. Do you still defend your faith, better still, share it?

English comedian Archie Rice, in the play *The Entertainer*, as a middle-aged, discouraged, disappointed man, says to his children: "Old Archie, dead behind the eyes, sitting on his hands, he lost his responses." It is so easy for us to lose our sensitivity. It was out of a similar disenchantment that a Yale professor said, "I never consciously gave up religious belief. It was as if I had put my beliefs in a drawer, and when I opened it there was nothing there at all."

This is the way we lose our faith by treating it like a toy, an heirloom, an antique, an academic degree. Faith is not to be protected but proclaimed! Unless we use it, we lose it. As Paul indicated, faith is more than a promise. It is fulfillment, it is joy, it is involvement. It is more than giving assent to a body of religious dogma; it is conviction and commitment, adventure and action. I like the way Leonard Hodgson of Oxford phrases it: "The test of the genuineness of a man's belief lies in his readiness to act upon it."

Real faith is like a moon shot. It is most frequently born in company with others who share the vision and who are willing to offer themselves in its fulfillment. As psychiatrist Dr. Erich Fromm has expressed it: "Faith is not prediction of the future, it is the vision of the present in a state of pregnancy." Scripture is stippled with men and women who acted on their faith. Among them are Abraham, Moses, Enoch, Mary, Joseph, Paul, and Jesus!

As we come to the last verse of the eleventh chapter of Hebrews—faith's hall of fame—we read, "And all these, though well attested by their faith, did not receive what was promised, since God had foreseen something better for us, that apart from us they should not be made perfect" (Heb. 11:39, RSV).

Faith has a tradition of community.

Wells, England, is the home of one of the most magnificent cathedrals in Europe. Built in the twelfth and thirteenth centuries, largely under the inspiration of Bishop Joselyn, a scintillating story of consecration emanates from its construction.

There is never a good time to build a church! There is either a depression, a war, or inflation. And so it was in the twelfth century. Parishioners were aghast at the magnitude of the project. Ultimately, however, an ingenious plan evolved. Fifty workmen, representing various trades, volunteered their services to the church for twelve months. Fifty identical small homes were built around the cathedral site in which workmen lived. Each received a penny a day compensation. At the end of twelve months the first fifty were replaced by a second group of artisans who committed themselves to a like period of labor. And so it went until the cathedral was completed. Their love is haunting and condemning. The majority of those who received a penny a day gave it back to their church.

It is little wonder that the architecture of Wells Cathedral is universally known, for the great edifice is more than the dreams of men and the blending of skills. It is a symbol of spiritual consecration, the implementation of first love!

Love is not only something one remembers but also something he does. Love is a transforming style of life, a style so needed in today's crowded, choking cities.

2

On Being Faithful

PICTURESQUELY LOCATED FACING THE AEGEAN SEA AND protected from the northeast by an acropolis, Smyrna had grown into a sizable city when destroyed by Lydia. It lay waste for three centuries before Alexander the Great saw possibilities of rehabilitation. His successors witnessed its renewal. Hence the reference to the Church as having died and come to life was uttered in the context of what actually had transpired in the history of that community.

It is heartening to recall the struggles at Smyrna and the caliber of her leadership. Polycarp, early bishop of Smyrna, may have known acquaintances of Jesus. This courageous soul became a devoted disciple, writing letters of encouragement to congregations. Toward the end of his long and illustrious life he went to visit Anicetus, bishop of Rome, to discuss the proper date of Easter. While there, Romans arrested him. Refusing to pay homage to Caesar, he was taken to the arena where the proconsul demanded that he reverse his position, repent, and reproach Christ.

Again he demurred with words for which the noble martyr became famed: "Eighty and six years have I served Him, and He never did me any injury; how then can I blaspheme my King and my Savior?" Unable to bend his will, break his spirit or frighten him, the Romans bound the bishop and burned him at the stake.

Although Smyrna was probably twelve hundred years old by the time this congregation was established, it apparently had a splendid reputation. John's greeting is beautiful: "Do not fear what you are about to suffer. Behold, the devil is about to throw some of you into prison, that you may be tested, and for ten days you will have tribulation. Be faithful unto death, and I will give you the crown of life" (Rev. 2:10, RSV). He did not say "be relevant," "successful," "independent," "liberal," or "conservative." John simply said: "Be faithful!"

Thomas Jefferson conceived of a rural democracy wherein every American would be self-employed and educated. He also placed great promise on civic and personal virtue. But the nation he and his contemporaries envisioned no longer exists. Three of every four of us live in cities and work for others. Modern society challenges the faithfulness of Christians.

Urban life is not only a severe test of democracy—about which the Constitution has little or nothing to say—but also a severe threat to the survival and influence of the Church. Politically, educationally, and spiritually we are unequipped to cope with cities and, apparently, economically unwilling. Their very atmosphere, competition, and depersonalization contribute to indifference, arrogance, and a damning lack of understanding.

Urban churchmen need to be challenged at the point of their faithfulness to institutions—home, church, school.

Despite change, they are still the fashioning forces of society. Irrespective of unpopularity of the establishment—and there are abundant reasons for its resistance—without some form of organization, precious little could be accomplished in our world. Moreover, someone must pay the bills! This is not to approve the sins of monopoly and power. Institutional renewal is part and parcel of campus reform even as church renewal is intimately identifiable with community crisis. The Church has long been interested in reforming the world. Now it, too, must change if it would seriously challenge society. All revivals must start with individuals whose vision and spirit change institutions.

There is something irresistibly contagious about visible faithfulness. I am reminded of Napoleon's classical description of the French statesman: "Talleyrand is a silk stocking full of mud." Does this not describe too many of us? We are suave, polite, adroit at playing games and gaining advantage, but not consistently faithful in sharing the faith and maintaining integrity.

Waiting in a corporation office, I noticed two women chatting as they watched the clock approach quitting time. They wanted to leave but had to wait three minutes before punching out. They already had cheated at least ten minutes, as they had changed from their uniforms to street dress.

Faithfulness is an irreplaceable characteristic in employment. One should be loyal to his employer, his firm, vocation, and loved ones. Before a funeral, a member of the bereaved family called to ask that I say something warm about his father who had been ill a long time. "He was a good man, a member of your church and its board." Then choking with emotion, he added, "Dad was a postman for thirty-two years and a good one. Everybody on his route loved him." The comment spoke volumes! A man should be faithful in the performance of his tasks.

Nowhere is faithfulness more needed than in the Church. We seem to think that absenteeism is a characteristic of churchmanship, something to be expected. In point of fact, it is an impressive or dissuasive example, the most dynamic or defeating form of evangelism.

I was greatly moved by a casual comment from a churchman of international acquaintance during a ministers' institute. The gentleman lives in Princeton, New Jersey, but worships in New York City—seventy-five miles away. Although genuinely committed to the ecumenical movement, he endeavors to assist his communion and congregation when possible. When I asked why he traveled so far to worship on Sunday, he replied, "It is our closest church."

"Do you go very often?"

"Every time I'm home," he answered.

Think of fighting traffic one hundred fifty miles on the Jersey Turnpike to attend church. Anyone who demonstrates such obvious faithfulness is a mighty advocate of the Church and, from human standards, most deserving of the crown of life.

Urban churchmen need to be challenged at the point of their faithfulness in the distribution and dedication of talents and resources. The city affords convenient and comfortable hideaways.

Is not this the burden of our Lord's parable of the talents? He spoke of a man who, while preparing for a journey, entrusted his money to three employees, charging each to manage well. To one he gave five talents, to another two, and still another, one. While we normally refer to a talent as a specific grace, skill, endowment, accomplishment

—and it is—here the word is employed to convey a specific sum of money, roughly one thousand dollars.

From the story we gain pertinent insights: men are not equally endowed, nor do they possess the same amount of courage and initiative. When the master returned, he praised the man who gained five additional talents, even as he lauded the one who doubled two. His words of commendation were precisely the same: "Well done, good and faithful servant; you have been faithful over a little, I will set you over much; enter into the joy of your master" (Matt. 25:23, RSV).

However, the servant who failed to invest—use—what he had been given and who complained was reprimanded: "You wicked and slothful servant! You knew that I reap where I have not sowed, and gather where I have not winnowed? Then you ought to have invested my money with the bankers, and at my coming I should have received what was my own with interest. So take the talent from him, and give it to him who has the ten talents. For to every one who has will more be given, and he will have abundance; but from him who has not, even what he has will be taken away" (Matt. 25:26–29, RSV).

The point of the story is not success but faithfulness. God loves and rewards the faithful. Yet many go through life with the perverted idea that the man with a million dollars is really successful regardless of how he earned it, if at all, and the man with ten million is ten times more successful. Dr. Harry Emerson Fosdick once said, "Nothing so recedes like success." Measured by the Master of all truth and value, these millionaires may have failed, even as the one who was more interested in larger barns than in better people failed.

Faithfulness is an unqualified characteristic of the Christian. It is impossible for any institution to exist without faithful members and supporters.

As citizens, we need to reevaluate from time to time our faithfulness to the principles and practices of democracy.

As parents, we need to inventory our loyalties—marital vows, children, and those who shape their destiny.

As Christians, we need to ask: are we faithful to our religious heritage? Are we faithful members of the Church? One of the inescapable measurements of Christian faithfulness is the portion of our income given to the Church.

Urban churchmen need to be challenged at the point of faithfulness in interpreting and communicating the mission of Jesus Christ in a fractured world. Is Jesus merely a historical phenomenon or a personal Savior? Is he a dead prophet whose life is interesting to review or a living presence in the company of men?

Once we were quite sure what *mission* meant. We are no longer certain. Obviously it is not determined by geography, race, or denomination. Population of the Christian community is not keeping pace with population growth. Mission means meeting. It is the cultivation of awareness, sensitivity, compassion, adventuring with love. Some would call it presence in the world, encounter, involvement. It is seeking and sharing a new life style. As the late Karl Barth would say, the development of the "I-Thou relationship." Mission is constructive Christian action. Yet to act consistently one must be acquainted with world needs.

Although the Church is powerless to tax, draft, or coerce, it must generate a spirit of imperativeness in adherents to proclaim the good news of Bethlehem—indeed Jerusalem! In his book *The Search for a Usable Future*, Martin E. Marty says we must move from comfortable tradition and dialogue to contagious incarnation. The pilgrim church offers no utopia. New forms of worship, however intriguing and beautiful, will bring no panacea apart from personal commitment.

The heart of the gospel is: God lives, God loves, and he cares for you!

Certainly the urban church must speak to the world—it is the only one it can speak to—and it must speak in comprehensible idioms. Yet as Georgia Harkness maintains, "Christian faith does not stand or fall from its convergence with the prevailing mental climate of Hollywood or Harvard, of Washington or any other 'secular city.' If the churches were simply to echo secular thought, they would have nothing to say to the modern world that is not being said as well or better elsewhere." [1]

It is at this point that we frequently become discouraged if not disenchanted with the Church, because one simply cannot measure the spirit and devotion of a congregation by commercial criteria, secular standards. Love is the law and life of the committed community. Its deeds do not fit a computer! Each soul must be appraised, supported, blessed, not in terms of criticism or merit, but joyous grace.

The Christian has the difficult, often discouraging task of proclaiming love in a world ventilated with hate; joy in an environment tense with bitterness; hope in a day of arrogance, doubt, and death.

Early Christians focused on the power of the gospel to correct and direct life. They believed Jesus was the Messiah, the Savior, whose spirit and love were indestructible. The early church was more than a meeting place; it was the custodian of the faith, carrier of the good news from one family, one community, and from one generation to another. These humble though strong believers often assembled to have fellowship, break bread, and pray. They held their possessions in common. Christ was the center, fulcrum, and circumference of their lives. Even before Elton Trueblood referred to a Christian as one who, with all the integrity he possesses, knows Jesus as the most trustworthy fact of existence, they were preaching that truth.

The churchman's impossible mission is to proclaim the uniqueness, permanence, and availability of Jesus Christ in a world of weird sounds and sights. In our time it is not easy to be faithful to this vision, for there is much in life to contradict the power of love. And yet the only practical advice is to tell the story to one's neighbor and incarnate its timeliness. It is always an expensive experience.

Sister Jacqueline Grennan of St. Louis, now Mrs. Paul J. Wexler, who stirred the Roman Catholic church with her theories of education, tells a beautiful story in her book *Where I Am Going*. A young reporter missed a press conference during the administration of President John F. Kennedy. When he awakened to his oversight, he dashed to the White House only to meet departing reporters. He moaned to Press Secretary Pierre Salinger that he was through, finished—no man could make such a mistake and survive. At this point the president entered and inquired about the situation.

Embarrassed and emotionally upset the man told Mr. Kennedy what had happened. Smiling, the president suggested, "Suppose we do it again?" and without fanfare sat down and repeated his statement. No one knew of the incident except the young reporter.

If a difference is made in our indifferent world, professing Christians must be faithful to the mission of telling again the old, old story of Christ's love, even at the risk of repetition and the enervating price of precious energy.

Urban churchmen must be persistent in articulating faith

in life eternal. Life is too cheap today to be impressive. Greater dimension of its value needs to be demonstrated. We must have and keep a heavenly vision. I am not commending seances, cataclysmic experiences, and revival hoedowns, but faithfulness to ideals once cherished and practiced because of commitment to Jesus Christ. When Paul was on trial before King Agrippa, he stood tall and his haunting words have echoed down the corridors of time: "Wherefore, O King Agrippa, I was not disobedient to the heavenly vision" (Acts 26:19, RSV).

Christian faith has a different meaning to each of us. This is the uniqueness of genuine faith; it does not divide, it unites. Faith to some means believing what others know is false. Others think that having faith means to be devoid of doubt. Most religious truths are debatable. Even the existence of God cannot be satisfactorily communicated to all. Faith is not something that can be packaged and coded and run through a computer with absolute accuracy; nor is it something that can be switched on and off like television.

At deeper levels a man's faith is reflected not only in what he says but also by what he believes and does. As Paul put it, faith is the substance of hope. The late Samuel Butler said, "You can do very little with faith but you can do nothing without it." Faith is never an isolated experience, never an award for Sunday school attendance. It is betting one's life on Jesus Christ.

Maintaining this stance in a world at war is not easy. Each of us must discover his own way of perpetuating the spiritual glow in these frightening days, keeping the vision and practicing his presence.

When Pope Paul VI visited India in 1964, he left his white Lincoln convertible for Mother Theresa—a nun who goes about in a fifty-cent sari and sandals. This humble person caught the vision of compassion when she was quite young and followed it from her native Yugoslavia to India. Over the years she and her colleagues have rescued from the streets and dumps of the cities more than twenty-one thousand dying persons. One horribly neglected man said to Mother Theresa, "I lived like an animal and . . . now I am dying like a human being. . . . Why?"

This saintly nun believes we see Christ under two forms. "We see Him on the altar—as bread, and we see Him in the slum, as the broken bodies of forgotten people."

This living encounter which gives shape and substance to hope is beautifully told by Paul Tournier, the noted Swiss theologian-physician. He shares an experience from participating with professional men who meet to explore ways of improving their skills and increasing their faith. On this particular occasion the man leading the discussion was a psychiatrist who confided that the problem of death had occupied his mind for months. While he realized they frequently discussed death in general terms and was aware of the cycle of interest—sex, love, vocation—he said, "Ultimately the problem of death takes first place and must be faced honestly."

Then the psychiatrist confessed he had been worrying about his own death. In fact, he had dreamed about it the night before. "In my dream," he continued, "I saw myself here, in this group. Paul Tournier was sitting beside me. He leaned toward me and said gently: 'Don't think only of death in general, nor of your death, but of his death. . . .' And I realized that he meant the death of Jesus Christ."

Dr. Tournier declares that suddenly the person of Jesus rose up in their midst. He was no longer an abstract figure, but very near and real.[2]

Our contagion and strength come from encounters with Christ—the source of faithfulness. This should be the business of the Church—introducing individuals to Jesus Christ.

The admonition to the congregation in Smyrna is the continuing directive to the Christian community: "Do not fear what you are about to suffer. Behold, the devil is about to throw some of you into prison, that you may be tested. . . . Be faithful unto death, and I will give you the crown of life."

3

On Being Too Tolerant

PERGAMUM WAS A BEAUTIFUL AND PROSPEROUS CITY THREE hundred years before Christ. Archeological diggings indicate that its public structures were phenomenal, its temples elaborate, and its hillside theater would accommodate thirty-five hundred people. Capital of the Roman province of Asia, legend has it that the city was founded by a son of Hercules. It was a place of wealth and culture which housed one of the finest libraries in the world, some believe upwards of two hundred thousand volumes; immense when one realizes that these were scrolls and not bound books.

Moreover, Pergamum was a health center, featuring a healing shrine dedicated to the god of medicine, Aesculapius, whose symbol was a serpent and who invisibly presided over orgies intermingled with worship. A temple dedicated to Zeus, the chief deity of the Greeks, also stood in Pergamum, as did one to Athena, goddess of wisdom and of women's artistry. A statue of Apollo, god of sunlight, prophecy, and the arts, lifted its head in the proud community to add indiscriminate blessings on all who came seeking health.

Balaamism also flourished. Balaam was a strange biblical character of whom Erskine said:

> To good and evil equal bent,
> And both a devil and a saint.

Balaamism attempted to make the best of both worlds. This weird combination of licentious dances and ritualistic meals around rustic altars attracted many.

As if Satan's complex was not sufficiently complete, Pergamum prospered from the philosophy of life represented by the Nicolaitanes. This bigoted class ruled over a large segment of the people. Their separateness, their practice of priest-craft, identified the Church so closely with the world that it could offer little more than hypothetical salvation. The Nicolaitanes ignored the power of the Holy Spirit; the message of Christ was always contingent upon their vote. Consequently, declared believers in Pergamum were too tolerant, permissive, lax, too closely identified with Satan's legion to be effective servants and contagious Christians.

Here is the charge: "I know where you dwell, where Satan's throne is; you hold fast my name and you did not deny my faith even in the days of Antipas my witness, my faithful one, who was killed among you, where Satan dwells. But I have a few things against you: you have some there who hold the teaching of Balaam, who taught Balak to put a stumbling block before the sons of Israel, that they might eat food sacrificed to idols and practice immorality" (Rev. 2:13–14, RSV).

Another problem facing the church in Pergamum concerned the sacrifice of animals. When ancient worshipers made a sacrifice to an idol, the priest usually cropped only the forelocks to burn. The animal then was divided: a portion to the priest, most of it to the owner, who thereupon would invite his friends to join him in a convivial feast. This hilarious celebration, associated as it was with ambivalent gods, posed serious questions for those who wanted to participate in the Lord's Supper.

What a setting for a church! This ancient city—crowded with pagan temples, idols, immorality, corruption, segregation, and conformity—is hauntingly contemporary. Aware of the situation but seeing the Church in Satan's bivouac, John was proud of its steadfastness. Antipas' martyrdom was not forgotten. Aware of their fraternization with evil, the writer warned them to repent. He promised that those who experienced renewal would overcome and be fed with "hidden manna" and receive "a white stone" with a new name inscribed upon it.

The American city is little better or worse than Pergamum. Not that Satan's cunning is confined to the city, but it is certainly more obvious and varied; his evil is more alluring. However discouraging and difficult, the Church must prove that integrity and love can conquer the city! It must demonstrate the style of Christian love, the therapy of forgiveness, the power of hope!

I have always appreciated Edgar A. Guest's comment that there is something inspiring about the sight of a church in a crowded city, a building surrounded by commerce and competition that has nothing to sell, but everything to offer.

Are not professing churchmen too tolerant of themselves? They have interesting ways of justifying action and equally intriguing rationale for inaction. The hard commands of Jesus are frequently ignored: "Go, sell what you have," take up a cross and "follow me," "love your neighbor," "be perfect." They add their own phrases: "In the old days . . . ," "the Church is not what it used to be . . . ," "I am sorry to see the church cut program, but . . ." Too few are sufficiently sorry to make constructive contributions.

Christians, especially sophisticated urbanites, are very tolerant of themselves and have clever ways of protecting self-interests. Jesus said the way to save life is to lose it, and the sure way of losing it is to embrace sneaking little schemes for saving it. When one attempts to make life too easy, he loses muscle tone, spirit, vision.

During the U.S. Open Tennis Tournament in the summer of 1968, Lt. Arthur Ashe was asked how he managed to serve an ace when he needed it. The brilliant player replied, "Mainly I think it's because people expect you to. . . . You've done it before and they think you can do it again. It's a kind of self-fulfilling prophecy."

The individual who is satisfied with his performance, too tolerant, too easy on himself, will not be able to serve the ace when he needs it. The disciplined life has a miraculous way of rising to the expectancy and needs of others.

Are not professing Christians too tolerant of American manners, mores, and morals? Are they not too tolerant of obscene and abusive language? Are they not too tolerant of exploitation? Like ancient Pergamum, modern cities are moral swamps.

Through today's diseased and dying cities creep peddlers and pushers of every conceivable illegal and harmful drug. Added to this perniciousness is a wave of experimentation with free living, the pad approach to sex so reminiscent of the Graeco-Roman world. One of the strange phenomena of that magnificent culture was that it looked upon prostitution as a necessary and acceptable style of life. Demosthenes counseled: "We have prostitutes for the sake of pleasure. We have concubines for the sake of daily cohabitation. We have wives for the purpose of having children legitimately and of having a faithful guardian of our household affairs."

Cicero described the debased moral code of the Romans by reminding his contemporaries that those who forbade young men to employ prostitutes were extremely severe. The distinguished statesman only echoed the accepted life style of his day, a style also common in Pergamum and in your city and mine.

And there is liquor. Never have Americans been so attractively badgered to drink as they are today. Glamorization of this evil is adroitly projected in advertisements associated with sex and success. The retail intoxicant beverage business in the United States runs upwards of fifteen billion dollars a year. This is a powerful economic fulcrum and a persuasive voice in the corridors of legislative and private power.

There are those who estimate excessive drinking costs America thirty-five million dollars a year in medical services; thirty million dollars in jail maintenance; one hundred million dollars in accidents; and at least five hundred million dollars in income losses. The medical director of Bethlehem Steel reports that alcoholism costs American industry two billion dollars annually in absenteeism. Other sources indicate that business mistakes attributed to intoxicated executives cost the nation seven and a half billion dollars a year.

In addition to the monetary, physical, and human waste associated with drinking is the irony that church people are involved. I am not sure if the New Testament teaches abstinence or temperance, but I am confident the Lord never intended his followers to waste their substance, health, and time in drunken debauchery.

Freedom is vanishing; the rule of law, deteriorating. Respected traditions and mores are questioned; permissiveness is encouraged. Much is being said about "new morality," "situation ethics," "existential action." To be sure one must have perception, compassion, and will to respond instantaneously to need, but one must also have orientation in Christian understanding of morality, decency, knowing what is basically right and wrong, if he is to be strong and effective in the Church.

We still have to wrestle with William Faulkner's comment in *The Wild Palms:* "If Jesus returned today we would have to crucify him quick in our own defense." We are much too fond of the civilization we have worked and sacrificed so to create in our image, to be threatened by the teachings and example of a small-town Carpenter.

Christians are too tolerant of the Church. Are they not satisfied with it as it is? Inevitably fallible individuals transmit the weaknesses of culture and discipline into the visible Christian fellowship. There is not enough distinction between the average church and club to make much difference!

One needs to see the creative role of the Church in this complex, corrupt, and challenging society. In her prologue to *From the Ashes of Christianity*, Mary Jean Irion tells of visiting a friend whose country home had been destroyed by fire. With dramatic delicacy she relates what it was like to move through the rubble of once beautiful furnishings now consumed and charred. Her friend, managing a smile, said, "Everything's gone, but they were only things. When we think about almost losing Mark . . ." Then she told the terrifying experience of rescuing her child at midnight.

As they walked amid destruction, her companion announced they would build again; that the foundations were solid. "We have already named the new house 'Phoenix.' Isn't that a wonderful name?" That, of course, is the bird of Egyptian fable that soars above ashes and defies death.

The cathedral of the mind has endured many intellectual catastrophes in the past centuries. Neither the visible nor the theological church of our fathers stands as it once did, but it nevertheless stands. There are, as Mrs. Irion says, two strains of people in the Church, indeed within churchmen themselves: the dogmatic and the dynamic. How the world needs dynamic Christians!

During days of revolutionary change, as one sifts through the ashes of concepts and convictions, pronouncements and accomplishments, it could well be that a new and more glorious Church will rise from the conflagration of criticism and indifference. Everyone knows the Church is but a shadow of its authentic self, but not everyone is willing to admit he is too synthetic to give it strength. Unlike the latter years of Queen Elizabeth who was so sensitive to her personal appearance she seldom had heart to look at herself in the mirror, one needs to accept the fact that church renewal must begin with its members, that structure is powerless to reproduce renewed spirit.

Robert A. Raines relates a stimulating experience in *The Secular Congregation.* It concerns two young ladies who came to First Methodist Church, Germantown, Pennsylvania, to hear a representative from the Southern Christian Leadership Conference. This was in 1963. One of them was an editor, the other an English physician taking an additional year's training in Philadelphia. They were intrigued by what they saw and heard even though they were somewhat hostile to the Church. Later they identified with the Germantown congregation. Although the young doctor had been considering an offer from a Nigerian hospital and the writer had applied to the Peace Corps, eventually the perceptive and creative young women decided to do mission work in their own community—an area called Wister.

These earnest Christians, searching for the meaning of life, meeting regularly for Bible study and prayer, found their answer. They bought a house in a depressed area that was 60 percent Negro. Members of First Methodist Church renovated the property. Covenant House, as it was called, afforded fellowship, visitation, and general assistance. Shortly after the young Christians moved in, there was a knock at the door. A woman asked, "Is it true that two white girls have bought this house and are going to live here?"

"Yes," answered Mrs. Raines.

"Why?" asked the stranger.

"Well, they wanted to live in an integrated area, and one of them who is a doctor hopes to start a medical practice here in the house."

Whereupon the woman shook her head in amazement and exclaimed, "My God, I can't believe it! Maybe this neighborhood's got a chance after all." [1]

From that simple beginning, Covenant House has become a place of encounter and assistance in the community; the embodiment of secular evangelism; literally Christ at work in the city. Christians must see to it that every neighborhood and individual has a chance to grow in grace and service.

I was impressed by a penetrating sentence from President Nixon's 1969 statement in Berlin: "I have a message for you. You are not alone."

Those who live and struggle with problems of the city church should remember they are not alone. Christ continues to weep over the city; he agonizes over the conditions of his children. Remember the promise to the church in Pergamum: "To him who conquers I will give some of the hidden manna, and I will give him a white stone, with a new name written on the stone which no one knows except him who receives it" (Rev. 2:17, RSV).

Whatever this beautiful and mysterious sentence communicates, it reminds each believer he is expected to participate in the struggle and that he who is victorious will receive an eternal reward. God reigns!

In a day of permissiveness and psychedelic dress, of beards and beads, sandals and boots, strange medallions and wild shirts, every Christian should strive for a white stone!

4
On Holding Fast

THYATIRA WAS A SMALL TOWN COMPARED WITH EPHESUS and Pergamum, located in the district of Mysia. This military outpost probably emerged about 290 B.C. It was strategically situated for the surveillance of enemies and to notify the capital city of possible attacks. The community was also known for its fabrics, wools, and dyes.

Thyatira, presumably established by Seleucus, was the home of Lydia, Paul's first convert in Europe. The courageous apostle met this woman during his mission to Macedonia. She and her companions were converted and baptized. Lydia was referred to as "a seller of purple goods." She was apparently a well-to-do businesswoman who catered to the elite. Nevertheless, after her conversion she told Paul, "If you have judged me to be faithful to the Lord, come to my house and stay" (Acts 16:15, RSV). She opened her home to the missionaries. Indeed, a church was started in her house.

We have no idea as to how many in Thyatira were of

Lydia's commitment. To the contrary, we know at least one contemptuous woman, Jezebel, was not. She claimed to be a prophetess, practiced fornication, and encouraged believers to eat food sacrificed to idols. She had many followers. Aware of the community's problems, also the caliber of many of its Christians, John condemned some for their immorality and commended others for their perseverance in things of the spirit: "I will lay no further burden upon you, except that you hold on to what you have until I come" (Rev. 2:25, Phillips).

What a glorious sentence of great wisdom, perennial advice lest the Christian community become a compromising church. It is always easy, particularly for churchmen, to quit, to give up too soon, surrender to conformity and evil. Every city is saturated with peculiar problems and devastating sins. John saw corruption flourishing in Thyatira. He urged the church to hold fast.

Christians need to hold on to their eagerness. When Americans go to sport events they are partial, responsive, vocal. Politically, citizens are expected to determine party affiliation and then openly and enthusiastically support their candidates. When they go to the movies, their emotions are exploited from the moment they enter the theater. However, when Americans go to church, behold a miracle: they freeze and change personalities! Aggressive, patriotic, energetic, sensitive people become indifferent, apathetic, and stoically silent.

I am not recommending that Christians wear their feelings on their sleeves, as do many; that they become so emotionally brittle that they surrender when the going is hard, or explode under pressure. But I am suggesting that they seek to capture that sense of aliveness, freshness, and emotional joy characteristic of pilgrims.

Anne Morrow Lindbergh and her distinguished husband

visited Cape Kennedy and had lunch with a number of astronauts, including the crew of Apollo 8. According to the report, they talked frankly and objectively about the hazards of flight to the moon: difficulties in navigation, the necessity of finding the narrow reentry corridor to earth. "One has the impression of keen, honest minds," continued Mrs. Lindbergh, "sensitive perceptions, relaxed bodies and eager spirits." What a perceptive comment! If only it described Christ's explorers and emissaries.

The late Vince Lombardi surprised the sporting world by returning to coaching professional football, the Redskins. After assuring his interviewers he was not a "miracle man" and that he could not "walk across the Potomac River," he went on to say, "I'm not ashamed of crying. Football's an emotional game. You can't be a cold fish and go out and coach. If you're going to be involved in it, you gotta take your emotions with you, mister."

A criticism of religion is that it is too emotional. The assertion is made that many are swept into the Church by intoxicating wizardry and emotional osteopathy, rather than being converted to Jesus Christ. Possibly in the past, but one would be hard-pressed to substantiate such a claim today. Americans are much too sophisticated to reveal feelings at worship. I am pleading not for shouting and stomping to accompany what a believer may interpret to be the entrance of the Spirit, but for sensitivity, awareness, an emotional response to people, Christian contagion, not predetermined sensationalism.

I was impressed by a comment heard in Monrovia a few years ago concerning President William V. S. Tubman. Above criticisms came the clear report that he was so aware of his people that if a boy in the bush "stubbed his toe, the president would say 'ouch!' "

Churchmen need to hold on to their courage. This is

a frightening and frustrating world. Tensions, proposals for protection against nuclear attacks, domestic turmoil, deterioration of law and justice, the fear of failing, disease, death, all test the mettle of Christians.

Cameos of courage are stimulating and suggestive of character. The courage of an athlete going into a championship contest is enviable, as is that of the paraplegic persistently going through his daily therapeutic treatments. The sheer nerve of astronauts and aquanauts is beyond description. There is the courage and concern of VISTA workers in ghettos, a parent trying to communicate integrity to his child. Self-reliance of a paratrooper dropped behind enemy lines has always demanded my admiration, but so has the quiet perseverance of a woman who lives alone and operates her home from a wheelchair.

In *Man, the Believer in an Age of Unbelief* the late Samuel H. Miller declared that the critical step in realizing selfhood was learning to live at the level of the soul, "an act which requires great courage." This eminent and stimulating preacher continued, "To become a soul is to reckon with the continuous crisis of becoming."

Dr. Miller's language is similar to that of Dean Charles R. Brown of Yale Divinity School who declared the Christian life might be described as the process of becoming, becoming sons and daughters of God. This is what the evangelist in the fourth Gospel meant when he wrote: "But to all who received him, who believed in his name, he gave power to become children of God" (John 1:12, RSV).

Reflect on the courage of a child: falling and rising again, walking in the dark, forever being introduced to new worlds. At last he goes to school. Imagine the misgivings and fears of that first day.

Life is a continuous drama of courage. It requires considerable will to answer the call of vocation. It inevitably forces one to inventory himself, evaluate liabilities and assets, and determine the degree of commitment. The courageous soul is not one who knows no fear; he is one who is willing to assume risks in attaining worthy objectives irrespective of danger.

In reading the life of Jesus, one cannot escape the quiet, persistent quality of his courage. From his initial encounter with belligerent hometown dissenters to walking into the establishments of power and injustice in Jerusalem, there was a singleness of purpose that dominated his life and drove him forward without flinching.

The Christian does not have visible envoys and attachés. He, too, is exposed to exploitation and death. Physical, mental, moral stamina has always characterized a cross-bearer at his best. Like Luther, facing his moment of truth, saying, "Here I stand, I cannot do otherwise," every believer must find his place of integrity and stand. The churchman must have the courage to make choices, decisions, commitments that will contribute to a constructive difference in today's hostile world.

Analyzing certain British victories over the French, the Duke of Wellington said, "British soldiers are not braver than French soldiers, they are only brave five minutes longer." The Christian, whether in Thyatira, Cleveland, or Los Angeles, is challenged to be brave longer than his enemies.

Churchmen need to hold on to their hope. No civilization or individual has long endured without the stimulant of the indispensable ingredient called hope. One of the encouraging notes in President Nixon's report on his 1969

European visit was "hope"—hope of reviving genuine expressions of communication and trust, hope of creating more tempting alternatives to war.

Hope is not a common signature today, yet it is one of life's intangibles that generates balance, power, and drive. It has always been man's desperate dream. St. Paul declared man is saved by hope, then quickly added, "Now hope that is seen is not hope. For who hopes for what he sees?" (Rom. 8:24, RSV). Man is challenged to separate hope from magic, reality from fancy.

Martin Luther believed that everything worthwhile in life was accomplished by hope. Samuel Johnson, Britain's brilliant man of letters, said, "Where there is no hope there can be no endeavor."

Dr. Ernest Gordon, World War II hero, dean of the chapel at Princeton and author of *Through the Valley of the Kwai*, declares that when prisoners were brought into camp, some were just bodies, marked for death. "They had lost their hold on life."

All live by hope. The pregnant wife hopes the baby will be normal; the father hopes he will be able to provide everything necessary for the child's development. A student hopes he will graduate, if not with honors, at least not at the foot of his class. A prisoner hopes for reprieve; the farmer hopes the seasons will be favorable. Parents hope the mail will bring word from scattered children. The pastor hopes his people will become more responsive to the mission of Christ. Hope, as John Sutherland Bonnell says, "is a day-by-day tonic and inspiration."

Dr. Karl Menninger provides a helpful distinction between optimism and hope. Optimism, he says, always implies some distance from reality, while hope is more immediate. Hope is humble, modest, and unselfish. It embraces calculated risks, yet remains confident.

Some years ago a strange case was heard in the Court of Special Sessions, Brooklyn, New York. Mr. Harry P. Purvis, a local businessman, was charged with violating a community law by placing a sign on top his building advocating peace through world federation.

The advertisement was objectionable. Citizens brought charges against Mr. Purvis. They rested their case on an ordinance which declared that no firm should advertise anything on its property that was not available on the premises.

One of the chief witnesses for the defense was distinguished editor of the *Saturday Review*, Norman Cousins. Nowhere, he pointed out, did the ordinance specify that what was advertised had to be material. He asserted it was so rare few would recognize it. The product, he said, was hope!

Like inhabitants of Thyatira, Christians need to hold on to their faith in Jesus. "Faith is the assurance of things hoped for, the conviction of things not seen" (Heb. 11:1, RSV).

Life moves forward or deteriorates in proportion to Christian faith which always includes action. Faith is not an extracurricular activity of a churchman. It is not an honorary degree for joining the Church; faith is active acceptance of Christ.

Mature faith is personal. It cannot be inherited or purchased. It must be earned, it must be developed, for nothing is more essential on this journey through joy and pain than to be able to face life and death with courage and confidence, knowing that God cares and bestows. Life is a journey, not a debate.

Faith, as the late D. T. Niles declared, is "learning to live with God's delays." Jairus came to Jesus beseeching help for his ill daughter. On the way they were detained.

A suffering woman touched the Master. He stopped to identify with her, indeed to assist. Doubtless Jairus felt like telling the Great Physician to hurry. Meanwhile messengers arrived with word that the child had died. Jairus concluded it was too late!

Seeing the faces of the anxious people, the Lord turned to the distinguished man of the synagogue and said, "Now, don't be afraid, just go on believing!" (Mark 5:36, Phillips). The story does not end with conversation, but with a miracle. Jesus raised Jairus' daughter from the dead.

Regardless of failure, discouragement, inexplainable circumstances, the admonition continues—go on believing! This is God's world and he will have the last word, perform the last miracle.

The encouraging voice of the Spirit continues to speak to Christians in the city, "Hold on to what you have until I come!"

5

On Staying Alive

A PIONEER IN THE FIELD OF TRANSPLANTS, DR. CHRISTIAN Barnard of Cape Town, famed South African surgeon, was interviewed on nationwide television. In discussing his celebrated patient, Dr. Philip Blaiberg, the moderator asked, "What is his general attitude toward life?" The famous physician answered that Dr. Blaiberg had been so close to death that "he truly appreciated the miracle of life."

Each year a minimum of twenty-seven million Americans enter hospitals in search of health. Total cost of medical care in the United States per annum is approximately fifty-three billion dollars. It represents 5.9 percent of the Gross National Product, 7.5 percent of all personal incomes.

Rare diseases requiring highly specialized physicians and sophisticated equipment are frightfully expensive. We are entering an era of major and multiple transplants. A patient in New York provided several vital organs to different people in the city. This will be a growing practice, eventually intercontinental.

To escape fatal illness, the carnage of our highways, or obesity is indeed an accomplishment. To survive a day in cluttered, polluted, reckless cities is to substantiate the fact that the miracle of life is more mysterious than the miracle of death.

Institutions, like individuals, also struggle with the problem of staying alive. A friend, knowledgeable in college administration, declared a southern university with considerable prestige is facing financial catastrophe, a common plight of many schools today. This particular institution is already funding much of its program from reserves. Unless additional sources of income are soon found, the school will have not more than twelve years to live.

Businesses die. There are from eight to nine thousand failures a year. Not shocking news unless you were involved in an irrecoverable financial loss.

Churches are not immune to disease, failure, and liquidity because they, too, are comprised of vulnerable people subject to all the temptations, viruses, and moods of men, even death.

This was precisely the predicament that provoked the admonition to the congregation in Sardis: "I know all your ways; that though you have a name for being alive, you are dead. Wake up, and put some strength into what is left, which must otherwise die!" (Rev. 3:1–2, NEB).

Sardis was the prestigious capital of ancient Lydia. The proud metropolis, known for its wealth and wisdom, was considered an impregnable fortress because of its construction and its location between the slopes of Mount Tmolus and the gold-flecked river of Pactolus. Like beautiful San Francisco, Sardis resembled a well-planned citadel.

There are no indications that the church in Sardis had physically deteriorated, was in a "blighted community," or was insolvent. Nothing is said about visible attrition. Considering its affluence, one may assume members were well housed, nicely dressed, and capable of performing their rituals with considerable grace. Decadence was due to spiritual disintegration. The congregation had become a well-guarded island of serenity and exclusion. Their chants had lulled them to sleep. They were dying with dignity! Not all professing Christians in Sardis were faithless, but enough to warrant the stirring command, "Wake up!"

Churches become irrelevant and ineffectual from many causes. Some would rather die than rediscover truth or scrap tradition. Some die because they are too rich; some because they are too poor; others because members are unwilling to work; still others because they ignore worship. Some fail from lack of spiritual resources; others because they attempt to substitute knowledge for faith. Some congregations are caught in sociological and population shifts which discourage, if not provide additional excuses to marginal members. Attrition gradually consumes the visible body.

External conditions, however, are never as perilous as internal inertia. There are those who feel the Church is more committed to itself than to the world. When this occurs, death results from what Arnold Toynbee calls "failure of nerve." Jesus did not come to save the Church, but the world!

The ills of society will not kill the Church. There is standing room only in churches of Russia. Does austerity breed loyalty to Christ?

Unwillingness to be consistent servants of the Lord contributes to the ineffectiveness and death of the Church. God will save the Church without man's cooperation and commitment.

If the Church is to live, it must be obedient to the living Spirit. It must distinguish between an echo and a Voice; between success and total stewardship. It must recognize and accept its relationship to Christ. "I am the true vine, . . . Every branch of mine that bears no fruit, he takes away, and every branch that does bear fruit he prunes, that it may bear more fruit" (John 15:1–2, RSV).

However critical one may be of the visible church, impatient with its inability or unwillingness to implement the ideas and ideals of Jesus, wherever the Spirit of Christ is, there is the Church; where the Spirit abounds, there is no death. The Church is always more than a well-regulated institution; it is the people of God in frustration and pilgrimage, hope and joy, demonstrating the full life.

Edwin Markham, the American poet, once was asked his favorite quotation. He replied:

> That's the wise thrush; he sings each
> song twice over
> Lest you should think he never could
> recapture
> The first fine, careless rapture!

This is the continuing challenge of the Church, to recapture the spirit of Christ in alienated society, the spirit of joy that accompanies one at his work, produces music of faith, and keeps him concerned and sensitive to the needs of people.

The congregation at Sardis needed to recapture, rediscover its mission. They had admired themselves too long; they had been their own best followers; their careers were more important than their convictions. The brethren at Sardis needed a spiritual transfusion. Their religion was a well-regulated form that had lost its transforming power.

A continuing danger of American affluence is that observers will be unable to differentiate between western culture and Christianity. This is why some refer to our faith as a "crossless" Christianity; the Church, as they see it, is not the catalyst of renewal but a deterrent to change and compassion, equity and justice.

The psalmist sensed this temptation and prayed, "Cast me not away from thy presence, and take not thy holy Spirit from me" (Ps. 51:11, RSV). The word *Spirit* was variously used and interpreted among ancient folk. It ran the gamut from fear to frenzied ecstasy. The prophets associated it with righteousness. These men of God felt they were directed by the Spirit. They considered themselves liberators.

Jesus possessed a spirit which overshadowed law. There was confidence and joy in his style of living that attracted many and alienated others. He opened his ministry in Nazareth with the simple but compelling words, "The Spirit of the Lord is upon me, because he has anointed me to preach good news to the poor" (Luke 4:18, RSV).

The early church demonstrated power of the Spirit. When a congregation loses its sense of awe and of directing, supporting purpose, it is dead. It is no more than a theater with a pipe organ, a country club with a communion table! Conversely, when it is Spirit possessed, whatever the circumstances, location, there is commitment and victory.

During World War II, City Temple, London, was bombed twice in the spring of 1941. Roof gone, windows smashed, organ ruined, a sanctuary with a seating capacity of two thousand became a charred cameo of former days. Within a month after the first incendiary bomb exploded, another claimed what remained of the building. Yet all the while this courageous congregation, scattered over a wide area, full of the Spirit, continued in fellowship and worship, meeting wherever a place could be obtained. Its famous pastor, Dr. Leslie Weatherhead, declared they sensed their kinship with first-century Christians. Without despair but in great confidence and determination, he said, "We, the living members of the spiritual City Temple, 'Stand in the temple of our God as pillars—' "

The Spirit keeps the Church alive, not the statistics, additions, budgets reported to denominational headquarters.

If the Church is to live it must be obedient to its mission—communicate and demonstrate the love of God as revealed in Jesus Christ. What a difficult ministry in a hostile world! Like fire, this mission burns without consuming itself. It calls disciples from every country and city to participate in creating under God a united Church, "truly catholic, truly reformed, and truly evangelical."

Throughout the ages the test of the Church has been its spiritual temperature, its sense of mission and urgency. That amazing man, John the Baptist, standing between the Old and New Covenants, said, "I baptize you with water; but he who is mightier than I is coming, . . . he will baptize you with the Holy Spirit and with fire" (Luke 3:16, RSV).

Fire in the Old Testament was usually associated with sacrifice, fear, miracle. Jesus used the word to convey ability of the Spirit to consume, cleanse, purify, communicate. The simile reaches a glorious climax in the conflagration of joy and power on the day of Pentecost. "And there appeared to them tongues as of fire, distributed and resting on each one of them" (Acts 2:3, RSV).

Indeed the Lord declared that he "came to cast fire

upon the earth" (Luke 12:49, RSV). However difficult this passage, it generates the beauty, warmth, and necessity of a glowing fire. As Elton Trueblood has commented concerning the early church, poor sticks made a grand conflagration. "A good fire glorifies even its poorest fuel."

The writer of the Roman letter expressed it this way, "Let us keep the fires of the spirit burning, as we do our work for God" (Rom. 12:11, Phillips).

Blaise Pascal described his life-changing experience of November, 1654, in a single word *fire!* In the evening of May 24, 1738, John Wesley declared, "My heart was strangely warmed." Archbishop William Temple confessed that the faith of others rekindled his own.

Walter Russell Bowie wrote a provocative book entitled *Men of Fire.* From St. Peter to St. Francis, from Roger Williams to Albert Schweitzer, Bowie describes the eagerness of devoted men to serve the Lord.

The magnificent procession of those who have been evangels of fire and light, contagion and compassion, extends into the twentieth century. Each reader could add names of those who have fired his faith and work. In my case, Harry Emerson Fosdick, Ralph Sockman, John F. Kennedy, Martin Luther King, Samuel H. Miller, Norman Thomas, and Halford Luccock.

The Church of the living God is the Church of the continuing flame. Unlike a chemical combustion, holy fire does not consume; it illumines and inspires.

During the Morgan-Nooe lectureship at Vine Street Christian Church, Nashville, Tennessee, in the 1950s, Dr. Nels F. S. Ferré, lecturer, often closed with these words from an ancient prayer:

Come as the fire and burn,

Come as the wind and cleanse,
Come as a light and reveal.
Convict, convert, consecrate,
Until we are wholly thine.

If the Church would be relevant, it must faithfully practice the presence of Christ. No man lives apart from God, no Christian lives apart from Christ, no churchman lives apart from the Church. Prayer is a prerequisite for preparation and participation in the drama and miracle of renewal.

What place has prayer in the life of twentieth-century man? Is it a down payment or personal fulfillment? Is prayer a magic wand, an out-dated gimmick? Is it a rejection of intellectual attainment? Is prayer incompatible with scientific exploration? Is it a lazy man's substitute for work? Is prayer cajoling ourselves into a better frame of mind? At best, is not prayer a request for a miracle?

The English author H. G. Wells told of an archbishop who, feeling the need of spiritual sustenance, went into a chapel to pray. Kneeling before the altar he said aloud, "O God!" Immediately a voice answered, "Yes, what is it?" The old man dropped dead of shock. The trouble with this story, as many writers have indicated, is that no one knows what the bishop heard, if anything! This much is certain: we, too, would be sorely shaken if God answered all our prayers. One always runs the risk when praying of having his requests fulfilled. As Harry Emerson Fosdick has said, be careful what you pray for; you might get it.

However defined, accepted or neglected, Jesus was a man of prayer. His conversations, not about God but with God, were daily. Every crisis of his life was preceded by prayer. Among his last recorded words from the cross were, "Father, into thy hands I commit my spirit!" (Luke 23:46, RSV).

Christ also admonished his followers to pray. The promise of fulfillment is astonishing. "If you ask anything in my name, I will do it" (John 14:14, RSV). "And whatever you ask in prayer, you will receive, if you have faith" (Matt. 21:22, RSV).

Impressed, his disciples asked Jesus to teach them how to pray. His model prayer remains unexcelled and inspiring. Early believers met to meditate, break bread, resensitize their spirits and return to the world to resume the struggle.

Although the discipline of prayer—the pathway to God—may not bring the coveted miracle, immediately cure ills of the city, the Christian is challenged to continue conversations with God. Not that the Father needs to be reminded of human problems so much as man needs to be reminded of God's presence and power.

Jesus referred to the temple of worship as the house of prayer: where believing souls could confess their inadequacies, quietly or audibly make known their needs, and courageously recommit themselves to higher purpose.

A modern testimony is dramatically described by Stephen Verney in *Fire in Coventry*. This beautiful English cathedral was destroyed by a German blitz in November, 1940. A number of medieval nails were found in the rubble and scorched wood. Many of these were gathered up, plated, made into crosses, and distributed throughout the area, indeed the world. The largest of these crosses was set on an altar amid the ruins of the apparently dead church. Behind the altar was placed a larger cross of charred wood. Back of this and written on a wall were the words, "Father forgive." The Coventry Cross of nails became a symbol of forgiveness, the living presence.

Twenty-two years later, in 1962, a new cathedral was dedicated. Much of the world witnessed portions of the service on television. However, it was not generally known that the people of the diocese had concluded earlier that God wanted "not just a consecrated cathedral, but a consecrated people living round it." And so the bishop and his colleagues visited every parish, starting with the Monks Kirby Chapter in 1959, sharing the story, searching for truth and mission, praying and fellowshiping together, reaffirming their vows, and preparing themselves as a people to reenter the house of God.

Describing this new covenant, Stephen Verney wrote, "Our cathedral was burnt, and out of the ruins sprang new life. It had been a glorious piece of medieval architecture, where the love of God was preached and the praises of God sung. But it had to die before it could bear rich harvest." [1]

The Coventry story is a reminder that the cross is the breaking point in life, that there is no living Church apart from the Holy Spirit, love, and prayer. That which keeps alive the New Covenant is not only participation in his Supper of renewal and confrontation, but also witnessing to his living presence. Canon Verney concludes, "God is breaking us, so that He may give us to our fellow men." Coventry, believed by many to be dead, came gloriously alive!

There is a remarkable reference to Emperor Hirohito of Japan in John Gunther's *Procession.* In referring to the Emperor's puritan ways, demanding schedule, abstinence from drinking and smoking, Gunther says, "One curious item is that he is said never to wear any clothes twice, not even underwear." His used clothing was given to minor officials and considered a precious gift.

The faithful in Sardis were told if they conquered

they would walk with the Lord, not in hand-me-downs, but in special robes. Here is John's promise: "They shall walk with me in white, for they have deserved to do so. The victorious shall wear such white garments, and never will I erase his name from the book of life" (Rev. 3:5, Phillips).

6
On Being Obedient

TWENTY-EIGHT MILES SOUTHEAST OF SARDIS LAY THE CITY of Philadelphia. Founded about 140 B.C., this newer and less prestigious Asian center had little to distinguish it other than its restoration following the devastating earthquake of A.D. 17, which also claimed its chief deity, Dionysus. In gratitude for imperial assistance in rebuilding, it was known briefly as Neo-Caesarea, "the new city of Caesar." During the reign of Nero, the original name was restored.

The congregation in Philadelphia, like the one in Smyrna, was free of blame and censure. The angel to this church said: "Here is the message of the holy and faithful one who *has the key of David*, so that *when he opens, nobody can close, and when he closes, nobody can open:* I know all about you; and now I have opened in front of you a door that nobody will be able to close—and I know that though you are not very strong, you have kept my commandments and not disowned my name" (Rev. 3:7-9, JB).

Christians at Philadelphia believed God opened and

closed the significant doors of life. These ancient churchmen had proven their ability to be trusted with the gospel. They were not circumscribed by circumstances.

In a *Saturday Review* editorial, Norman Cousins projected how each member of society eventually becomes so enamored with the interests of his community that he often loses contact with the rest of the world. Cousins refers to such people as "prisoners of context."

Individuals reflect geography, vocation, prejudice! Recognizing this temptation, J. B. Phillips says in *Ring of Truth*, "Let the modern world conform to him [Christ], and never let us dare to try to make him fit into our clever-clever modern world."

The brethren in Philadelphia were peculiar in that they lived in a strikingly different city as contrasted with the more ancient and aristocratic communities of Ephesus, Smyrna, and Pergamum. Furthermore, citizens of Philadelphia lived in fear of another earthquake. They never knew when physical doors would crumble. Their demeanor was gentle, courage unquestioned, actions sincere, and loyalty enviable. Although limited in power, these inhabitants of volcanic fields were commendable disciples of Christ.

In a day of general permissiveness it is not popular to commend obedience, yet every profession, happy marriage, honor student, exceptional athlete, individual, knows there are limits to freedom.

Learning obedience is one of life's essential and inescapable lessons. The undisciplined child seldom attains his potential. A college girl who spends her summers working with emotionally disturbed children told me the major cause of their trouble was that many came from insecure homes with little discipline.

Dietrich Bonhoeffer proclaimed, "The road to faith passes through obedience to the call of Christ." Until one finds and follows this path, the invitation to become Christian is vague.

One recalls that General Washington complained his soldiers would not heed commands until explained. Laws of society must be obeyed if a nation is to escape anarchy.

In a landmark speech before the American Bar Association, St. Louis, August, 1970, Chief Justice Warren E. Burger indicated need for changes in judicial proceedings and policies. "In the supermarket age," he said, "we are like a merchant trying to operate a cracker-barrel grocery store with the methods and equipment of 1900."

Statutes and structures must be challenged and changed if the country is to maintain integrity and efficiency. It is imperative that proper procedures be respected.

In any age the good life depends on obedience to higher authority. Allegiance to God must take precedence over loyalty to man. After Nebuchadnezzar took Jerusalem, he instructed his ministers to seek out four young men of superior intelligence, strength, and character. Daniel, Shadrach, Meshach, and Abed-Nego were selected. One can imagine the delight and dilemma of the captives as they journeyed from Jerusalem to Mesopotamia. Quartered in the king's palace, the Hebrew lads were privileged to enjoy plush accommodations, eat at the royal table, drink from goblets brimming with rare wines. These young men were confronted by temptations demanding decision: Should they do the expedient thing, or should they be obedient to their training?

In this moving story we read, "Daniel resolved that he would not defile himself with the king's rich food, or with the wine which he drank" (Dan. 1:8, RSV). Little wonder this remarkable man was able to interpret mysteries, withstand punishment, and emerge triumphant. Daniel had learned obedience. In the midst of anguish he said: "Our God whom we serve is able . . ." (Dan. 3:17, RSV).

Peter and John greatly disturbed Jerusalem by declaring, "We must obey God rather than men" (Acts 5:29, RSV).

The congregation in Philadelphia was commended because it obeyed the call to patient endurance. It found and fulfilled every opportunity to witness.

The inevitable connection between congregation and community prompted the angel to the church in Philadelphia to declare: "Behold, I have set before you an open door, which no one is able to shut; I know that you have but little power, and yet you have kept my word and have not denied my name" (Rev. 3:8, RSV). Whether the open door was New Jerusalem being promised or evils of culture being identified, obedience to the gospel of Christ would ultimately prevail and enable believers to correct inequities.

A door is intriguing. Its design and coloring say "come in" or "stay out." There are times when it should be shut and times when it needs to be open. Nothing is more frustrating when one desires entrance to his home than a locked door, nothing more gratifying than an open one.

When William James, noted philosopher, was a little boy, he wrote a friend about their new summer home: "It is a wonderful house, with all the doors opening outward." The Christian life should be lived with openness. Too many of us live behind façades, barricades of mind and mortar. We have interesting ways of turning life inward.

Before delegates to the World Council of Churches arrived in Evanston, Illinois, 1954, the Chamber of Commerce, wisely attempting to prepare the community for the cultural shock of a multiracial conclave, urged citizens to forget their prejudices for seventeen days. Christians should forget pettiness forever.

Philadelphia was an open city lying between the ancient countries of Mysia, Lydia, and Phrygia. Those who created the community saw an opportunity to Hellenize travelers and tribesmen. There were no barriers; instead there were gates opening outward. The church had apparently adopted this philosophy and was practicing spaciousness of spirit despite its discouraging limitations.

Like individuals and communities, churches tend to become ingrown, protective, authoritarian. Yet the Church of God needs no protection. Its doors and windows must be open. Winds of God must blow through the structure as well as the souls of worshipers. Is not this what the Reformation was all about? Was not this the stance of John XXIII? Desire for spaciousness and consecration led Wesley to break with the Church of England and caused Thomas and Alexander Campbell to feel the church of their fathers spiritually too small; its doors opened inward.

Too often doctrines and attitudes close church doors. It is amazing how congregations sit in judgment on one another and establish man-made requirements for membership in and operation of God's institution.

Since I am more familiar with Disciples of Christ than other groups, permit me to illustrate this point by sharing two encounters with pulpit committees of large congregations.

In one situation the first question asked was, "Mr. Jones, are you solvent?" Although I could answer in the affirmative, and while I fully appreciate the implications of financial responsibility and integrity, can you imagine this being the foremost question of a pulpit committee? I could not possibly work in such a climate.

Another committee asked me how I felt about "open membership" (a Disciple term for inclusiveness; acceptance of transfers from other denominations without rebaptism). In response, I endeavored to explain: although committed to immersion, it could never be the only requirement for church membership. Moreover, anyone committed to Christ, who is trying to live the Christian life, who is satisfied with his mode of baptism, should be accepted into full fellowship in any church. However, I soon learned that no one could be a member of that congregation unless he were immersed, irrespective of Christian heritage, faith, or performance.

Regardless of local polity, the church in Philadelphia impresses one with its openness, spiritual spaciousness, and stamina.

The angel to the church in Philadelphia also promised the victorious ones they would be pillars in God's temple. What a simile! People, not pilasters, would be the permanent supports of the Christian community; people, not structure, would determine its destiny.

Human pillars, like giant trees, start from small beginnings. To excel is expensive. Stars and saints are grown, not born. Don Schollander, winner of four gold medals in the Olympics in Japan, who also performed well in Mexico, decided he wanted to be an Olympian when he was a lad. From age twelve he paid the price by swimming four to five hours daily.

Barbara Jo Rubin, one of the first women jockeys to ride in a major horse race, said she decided to be a professional rider "when I was a little girl and went to see *National Velvet*." A young man, when fourteen, said he wanted to be a physician. Today he is. A girl, graduating from high school, declared she aspired to become a nurse. Today she is.

The Church which Christ came to establish uses people as pillars, foundations, windows to reflect the example of Jesus in all fields of work and witness.

Visiting the gold mines of South Africa is an experience. The realization one is three miles beneath ground level is frightening. However, I was fascinated by the skill of men who shored up the earth with wooden supports although few could read or write. These humble men are pillars in the gold-mining business.

Archbishop of Montreal, Paul Emile Cardinal Leger, startled the religious world in 1968 by resigning from the largest Roman Catholic diocese to become a "simple priest" among African lepers. During that same year Gerald Kennedy, bishop of the United Methodist Church in California, accepted the pastorate of First Church, Pasadena. Brilliant men, at an age when most are interested in retiring to suntans, golf, and leisure, accepted new and demanding situations.

To those who are suspicious of men over thirty, note Archbishop Leger was sixty-three when he decided to go to Africa and Bishop Kennedy sixty-one when he accepted a pastorate. When asked why, the noted Methodist leader replied, "Because that is where the action is." Pillars in God's temple!

Three American missionaries—Mac Myers, pilot, Eunice Goodall, and Mary Hoyt—encountered flying difficulties in their Cessna 185 and crashed in the Northern Province of the Democratic Republic of Congo (Kinshasa) on October 13, 1968. The charred plane and bodies were found on Thanksgiving Day in the jungle north of Monieka. The victims were brought to Boende for burial. Mr. Myers was a United Methodist layman, Mrs. Hoyt, a Roman Catholic nurse and wife of a physician, and Mrs. Goodall, Disciple teacher and wife of a medical doctor.

Since they had been involved in ecumenical work, services of memory were all-inclusive. An attending missionary wrote me: "How better can a person leave this world than when he is where he wants to be and is doing the work he wants to do?"

These committed Christians will long be remembered as pillars in the Church. They had so much to give and they gave it all.

The angel to the church in Philadelphia promised the faithful they would receive new names. "I will write upon him the name of my God, and the name of the city of my God, the new Jerusalem" (Rev. 3:12, Phillips).

Names are intriguing and informative. A name is not only the appellation of a person, place, or thing; it is also the summation of reputation and character. Thus every person has two names: one designated by parents, the other, earned. One is recognized by signature or photograph; the other, by performance. One is that to which he answers; the other, that to which he aspires.

Our religious fathers were not only slow to name their children, waiting for character traits to emerge, but were also given to the beautiful custom of changing names after moments of religious ecstasy and victory.

If Laban is Scripture's Shylock, then Jacob is its Jekyll and Hyde. His life was one long struggle—as is every man's—between choices, between natures: one base, the other benevolent. As a youth Jacob was deceitful. He tricked his father and cheated his brother out of his birthright. Then, in exile, he encountered God. The event was so genuine the report refers to it as "wrestling." After a fitful night, a voice asked: " 'What is your name?' And he said, 'Jacob.' Then he said, 'Your name shall no more be called Jacob, but Israel, for you have striven with God and with men, and have prevailed' . . . Jacob called the name of the place Peniel, saying, 'For I have seen God face to face, and yet my life is preserved' " (Gen. 32:27–28, 30, RSV).

Consider Saul of Tarsus, brilliant, finely trained, a Pharisee of Pharisees, a pugilist who delighted in harassing and persecuting Christians. There came the day when this belligerent man, journeying toward Damascus, was blinded and fell to the ground in fear. Once again there was a voice: " 'Saul, Saul, why do you persecute me?' And he said, 'Who are you, Lord?' And he said, 'I am Jesus, whom you are persecuting; but rise and enter the city, and you will be told what you are to do' " (Acts 9:4–7, RSV).

This strong spirit was led to Damascus where he lived in blindness and without food or water for three days. His conversion was confirmed, his itinerary changed, and thereafter he was known as Paul, courageous apostle, missionary, and author of a cluster of New Testament letters.

Consider the "Big Fisherman," as rugged, strong, and smelly as his work. Yet Jesus recognized in this mountain of a man called Simon, character, truth, courage, and faith.

The record relates that when the Master was in the district of Caesarea he queried his disciples as to his identity. They answered, "Some say John the Baptist, others say Elijah, and others Jeremiah or one of the prophets" (Matt. 16:14, RSV). Jesus was not satisfied with the general answer, so sharpened the question saying, " 'But who do you say that I am?' Simon Peter replied, 'You are the Christ, the Son of the living God' " (Matt. 16:15–16, RSV). The Lord was impressed, pleased, and replied, "Blessed are you, Simon Bar-Jona! For flesh and blood has not revealed this to you, but my Father who is in heaven. And I tell you, you are Peter, and on this rock I will build my church, and the powers of death shall not prevail against it" (Matt. 16:17–18, RSV).

Character and faith have always distinguished strong men, men who determined history.

Identifications and transformations are common in Americana. Less creative than Hamilton, less learned than Jefferson, lacking Franklin's wit or Henry's eloquence, Washington was acknowledged master of them all in the superb balance of deed and thought. How appropriate that he should be known as "Father of Our Country."

When John Rockefeller III was born, he was not given the middle initial "D" but told when he felt he was able and ready to assume the responsibilities it suggested, the initial would be bestowed. After schooling at Harvard and Yale, teaching in Japan, serving in Job Corps, though still restless and uncertain of his future, he wrote his father that he wanted "the name and the responsibility."

I never cease to wonder at the trust and love involved in a wedding ceremony, where the bride surrenders her name for the one she loves. Linguistically the exchange is sometimes penalizing. Yet love is more interested in sharing than preserving.

Is not this the message to the church in Philadelphia? "I will write upon him the name of my God, and the name of the city of my God, the new Jerusalem. . . . I will write upon him my own new name" (Rev. 3:12–13, Phillips).

Jesus' visit to the country of the Gerasenes is pertinent and suggestive. Upon leaving the boat he met a madman who lived "among the tombs." It was not only a dramatic encounter but a symbolic reminder of man's persistence in living in the past, his itching tendency to cling to what is outmoded. The ill man had become such a nuisance that he was anonymous. He had lost his name. Hated and feared by his neighbors, he was frequently imprisoned.

Strangely enough, this frightful man ran toward Jesus crying, " 'What have you to do with me, Jesus, Son of the Most High God?' . . . And Jesus asked him, 'What is your name?' He replied, 'My name is Legion; for we are many' " (Mark 5:7, 9, RSV).

Above complaints and sorrow associated with the frightened swine that ran headlong into the sea, this cleansed and converted soul begged Jesus to permit him to follow. The Master refused, saying, "Go home to your friends, and tell them how much the Lord has done for you, and how he has had mercy on you" (Mark 5:19, RSV).

It is Jesus who writes his "own new name" on those who accept, obey, and serve him.

7
On Being Enthusiastic

LAODICEA WAS THE SEVENTH COMMUNITY MENTIONED IN the roll call of city churches in John's Revelation. Located near the intersection of three well-traveled roads, it was a commercial center, producing expensive cloth and attractive carpeting from native black wool. It could also boast of a medical school.

This flourishing city, founded by Antiochus in 250 B.C., was a success story. It was proud and prosperous. A heavy concentration of Jews added imagination and initiative. The church, like the community, endeavored to worship God and mammon simultaneously.

A Christian congregation existed in Laodicea in the days of Paul. In fact, he requested the Colossians and Laodiceans to exchange letters of encouragement and nurture. Some believe they may have received additional correspondence from the apostle, including his Epistles to the Ephesians.

Old "First Church," however, was dying. Its past was more intriguing than its future. Being content with surrounding conditions and security, it was insensitive to human need and the Holy Spirit. The word of warning from the Lord of the candlesticks was, "I know what you have done, and that you are neither cold nor hot. I could wish that you were either cold or hot! But since you are lukewarm and neither hot nor cold, I intend to spit you out of my mouth!" (Rev. 3:15–16, Phillips).

This is not poetical language. It is pointed, sharp, condemning. As is so frequently the case with comfortable congregations, Laodicea was proud of its history and wealth. But to them came this disturbing evaluation: "For you say, I am rich, I have prospered, and I need nothing; not knowing that you are wretched, pitiable, poor, blind, and naked" (Rev. 3:17, RSV).

Confident though they were, the Lord felt sorry for them. Despite finery, complacency, financial independence, they were spiritually poor. Smyrna was a rich, poor church; Laodicea was a poor, rich church. The former knew its mission; the latter knew only symbols and stations of accomplishment. Laodicea was neutral, insensitive, lukewarm. Awareness of the Spirit did not increase enthusiasm. This ancient congregation illustrates a comment from the late Dr. James Pike: "The poor may inherit the earth, but it would appear that the rich—or at least the rigid, respectable and safe—will inherit the Church."

One prevailing characteristic of this so-called Christian congregation was complacency, just as it is in Dallas, Denver, Miami, or your city. It exemplifies what Søren Kierkegaard felt about Christianity in general, namely, its unwillingness or inability to demonstrate relevant vitality.

The church at Laodicea had lost its decisiveness, ability to make moral and spiritual distinctions, pronouncements, and decisions. The atmosphere was not conducive to genuine worship nor its hospitality sufficiently warm to attract strangers to Christ. There was little of the cross in this church, even less of the resurrection.

This lukewarm, maudlin group of goodish people were indifferent to the fundamental truths of God and the directing spirit of Christ. They were undisciplined, uncommitted.

In his spiritual biography *Report to the Creator*, Jerome Ellison, whose confessions are reminiscent of St. Augustine, shares an experience from adolescence. One Sunday during worship the lad felt the visitation of the Spirit. He was so excited he could hardly wait for the benediction to discuss his feelings with adult members.

"To my complete amazement the grownups clustered into their customary little after-church talk-knots—and talked about utter trivia! As I sought for words and opportunity to introduce the only topic I thought really mattered, I was tongue-tied. Finally somebody noticed me and remarked that the boy looked pale. Somebody else said maybe church was too much for him, and everybody laughed. I was deeply offended and concluded that all adult church members were hypocrites."

This disillusionment led to long years of indifference, religious depression, nagging doubt, reading, and repenting. After much agonizing, Jerome Ellison returned to the Church. Complacency was still its obvious characteristic. Dignified people continued their rituals of worship. Though he suffered a repetition of his boyhood experience, happily he again encountered the Holy Spirit. As before, the congregation largely ignored him. "But now," he wrote, "I was an adult, I would not remain silent. Whenever there was opportunity I spoke, shouting, 'Look Who's here!' " [1]

Is there anything more discouraging than a congregation awkwardly, if not reluctantly, going through its morning calisthenics? Is there any nostalgia comparable to professing Christians who leave the impression the destiny of the Church coincides with their will and vote?

The spirit of Laodicea continues to characterize many American churches. Modern congregations, surfeited with pride, accomplishment, material security, sin, are frequently disquieting to the Spirit and discouraging to those who seek the Master.

In a society of development planning, lunar landings, economic controls, widening intolerance, how is the Church to become more meaningful, contagious, supportive, and enthusiastic?

Discipline dispels complacency. Discovery of high purpose and dedication to fulfillment are necessary conditions of enthusiasm, be it corporate or personal. If the Church is to be relevant, redemptive, it must seek to know and practice the will of God. Far from a static situation, it requires constant clarification of mission if a congregation is to be vibrant. It must be able and willing to differentiate between place and purpose, building and spirit.

Society is experiencing the inevitable results of permissiveness. Individuals demand their rights, but not enough accept their responsibilities.

There are two kinds of discipline: superimposed and self-imposed. The first is the hand of power, martial law, totalitarian tactics. The second, which requires much more maturity to achieve, is to develop a rational, responsible, and defensible style of life. It demands that one be as critical of self as of others. Self-imposed discipline is not inflexible nor does it kill the spirit of joy. In fact, it leads to an understanding of freedom and self. It engenders inward security and peace that make possible personal fulfillment.

However foolish it may appear, one admires the discipline and perseverance of the British physician who always dreamed of conducting a symphony orchestra. Not only did he live with this hope, but saved money, the equivalent of seven thousand dollars, with which he rented a hall and orchestra. Assuming the role of conductor, he said if the experiment proved satisfactory, he might abandon medicine. "I am now fifty-two and I don't have too much time left."

Paul said to Timothy: "Take time and trouble to keep yourself spiritually fit" (1 Tim. 4:7, Phillips). The simile is that of an athlete training himself after the example of the Lord. Spiritual discipline is more than rigid conformity to creed, diet, and daily habits. It goes beyond commitment to expressions of concern and deeds of love. The athlete does not train himself for the sake of conditioning, but rather for the privilege and joy of participating in the contest. God-given talent is one thing; the development of that gift is another.

I once heard Paderewski play the piano. I shall never forget it. When asked about his disciplines, he replied that if he missed practice one day, he could tell it; two days, his associates could detect it; and if he missed three days, his audience noticed it.

The living Church must provide some formula for regulation of one's spiritual life or it will be neither hot nor cold. An insipid church has no pulling or saving power.

One is reminded of a biographical note concerning the monumental witness of Dr. John Baillie. Three objects symbolized the wholeness of his life: the desk where he wrote, the chair where he read, and the pad where he prayed.

Renewal of hope, faith, and service generate enthusiasm.

It presupposes involvement. There is a difference between sideline and goal-line engagement.

Clarity of language addressed to those in Laodicea is a continuing challenge for personal and corporate renewal. "Those whom I love, I reprove and chasten; so be zealous and repent" (Rev. 3:19, RSV).

Renewal, says Elton Trueblood in *The Incendiary Fellowship*, like happiness, is rarely achieved by direct seeking. Persons seldom create; they discover what is noble and worthy in self-giving. Commitment is followed by hard thinking, work, and sacrifice. It begins with people who realize they are neither hot nor cold but who have been touched by and responded to the stirrings of the Spirit.

Every significant period of renewal in the history of the Church has involved movements of repentance. Renewal is impossible without repentance because repentance presupposes severance from old systems and sins and an earnest desire to put on the "new man." Repentance is always turning in a new and better direction.

Sir Henry Bessemer, responsible for a method of making steel, once declared he had an advantage over others wrestling with the problem, as "I had no fixed ideas determined from long established practice to control and bias my mind."

When this attitude is applied to the Church, it could mean that inexperienced churchmen, raw laymen, young adults, unsung clergy may see and correct signs of death in city churches even before so-called professionals.

Did not the Prophet of Nazareth see and expose the sins of the Temple before those trained in its nurture recognized or responded to their dilemma?

Did not the perception of a relatively unknown Augustinian monk challenge the practices of the Roman Catholic church, thus providing impetus to what is recognized as the Protestant Reformation?

Was it not a restless, unheralded missionary pastor who gave direction and depth to the Methodist movement?

Did not emigrants from Scotland, father and son, sensing denominational narrowness on the American frontier, desperately seeking Christian oneness with their colleagues, eventually initiate the movement known as Disciples of Christ?

Was it not a spindly Indian, educated in England where he observed and experienced discrimination, who later emancipated his people from British domination without firing a shot?

Was it not a black man from humble though Christian surroundings, weary from the serfdom of his people, who led the American civil-rights movement? By giving himself did he not add integrity to democracy, dignity and worth to all men?

The aching need of the church in Laodicea was enthusiasm. It continues today. Ours is an impersonal, calibrated world. Loss of enthusiasm is a constant danger in our technocratic society—a society that requires planning, control, expertise, and perpetual promotion.

Mrs. Ramsey MacDonald, wife of a former prime minister of Great Britain, said to her husband during the latter days of her life, "Whatever you do, put romance and enthusiasm into the lives of our children. With those qualities their lives will be good."

Enthusiasm is not synonymous with revolutionary slogans, pep rallies, and marches. Christian enthusiasm is rooted in and springs from a deep belief in the loving presence of Christ. Its most permanent manifestations are contagious examples of self-giving.

It is what David Soper calls "the thrust forward." It is none other than the Holy Spirit stirring the individual, directing, sustaining him through struggles of endurance and discipleship. The power is faith; the dynamic is love. This swelling, growing concern eventually consumes criticism and Christian claustrophobia, a style of life not easily acquired since it involves constant risks and exposure. Yet it generates enviable joy and stamina. "I can do all things in him who strengthens me" (Phil. 4:13, RSV).

Sad indeed are those who lose zest for life. It reflects on the Church. Not long ago the press reported the story of a young girl who committed suicide. She left this note: "I am twenty-one. I have seen everything worth seeing. I know everything worth knowing. I don't like life—it is cheap, dirty, disappointing. I've had all I want."

Contrast this fatal confession with that of the late Sir William Mulock, former chief justice of Ontario and chancellor of the University of Toronto, who was honored on his ninety-fifth birthday. The sprightly gentleman, speaking in tones that conveyed love for life, said, among other things, "I am still at work, with my hand to the plow, and my face to the future." This remarkable man lived to be one hundred years old.

In his stimulating and encouraging book *Enthusiasm Makes the Difference*, Norman Vincent Peale tells how Robert H. Schuller of the Reformed Church in America was sent to Orange County, California, to establish a new congregation. He was on a modest salary and had five hundred dollars for promotion. Enamored with the romance and challenge of building a new church, his enthusiasm was contagious. Eventually he leased a drive-in theater for Sunday morning services. He offered friendship and love.

Ten years later this missionary to California invited Dr. Peale to preach. He found a modern structure of steel and glass artistically placed in a twenty-acre plot of grass, flowers, and reflecting pools. Over the years the congregation has grown to three thousand members with an average Sunday attendance of four thousand. Dr. Peale participated in the groundbreaking service for "Tower of Hope," a ten-story structure which houses church personnel seeking to serve the total community. He reports that as he looked over the vast congregation, he realized enthusiasm was indeed "the powerful motivation to make things happen."

This is not the end of the story. A friend worshiped in Garden Grove Community Church the Sunday after Easter, 1969. According to the bulletin there had been fourteen thousand people present to celebrate the resurrection of Jesus. The forthcoming Sunday was to culminate a campaign to secure $500,000 for the purchase of ten additional acres of land. The pastor wrote in their bulletin, "We expect to announce a victory next Sunday morning. Come to church prepared to sing the Doxology!"

What a contrast to the spiritual temperature of Laodicea. A Christian must be a missionary of enthusiasm. He must bring a new throb to life, forever sing the Doxology with joyous integrity.

"If anyone has ears to hear, let him listen to what the Spirit is saying to the churches" (Rev. 3:22, JB).

THE SCENE

Within two hundred brief years leaven from thirteen colonies has fermented the most powerful country in the world. America has advanced from visible colonialism to a complicated system of freedom; from arduous labor to sophisticated machinery; from slow, painful travel to the inconceivable speed of a moon shot; from agrarian orientation to urban culture and corruption.

We are victims of a technological crisis. Machines threaten to annihilate their operators. Science has outdistanced man's willingness to detect and implement ethical and moral judgments. We have succeeded in sustaining man in outer space but have yet to accept changes and expenditures necessary to support him on earth. We have been more concerned with progress than with people.

America is facing grave and costly decisions. There must be a reordering of national and personal priorities. A single C–5A military airplane costs two hundred million dollars. Think of what that amount of money could accomplish in your community. The government can conduct studies, hold hearings, initiate programs, fund projects, but only the Spirit of God actively and contagiously at work in man can provide the city with hope and light.

Conservationists are so "up tight" about urban renewal, physical environment, that they sometimes forget moral and spiritual erosions which are even more devastating than general ecology. Never have human beings been exposed to so many pollutants of mind, body, and spirit. The city is a bizarre scene, a cinema of corruption, a weird marketplace of distorted values. Anyone who exploits the earth's resources, destroys the beautiful, pollutes human beings, sins against God and man. Life is a precious gift, not a retrievable experiment.

Evaluating space programs some years ago the American social critic and philosopher, Lewis Mumford, spoke prophetically: "Any square mile of inhabited earth has more significance for man's future than all of the planets in the solar system."

However you appraise the current scene, I am not one of those who believes the Church is irrelevant and that its ministry has collapsed. As Dr. James E. Dittes says, "the relevance of being irrelevant" is indeed an indication of the Church's vitality and integrity. The Church, discerning and responding to its deficiencies, is a unique harbinger of hope.

I cannot accept the allegation that churches are museums, buildings locked and unused during the week, constituting a drain on tax books and a visible contradiction of the gospel. I asked the administrator of an 1800-member congregation how many community organizations used their facilities during a year. He answered: "It was used 343 times this year." I cannot accept the charge that the Church is not involved in community.

If by Church is meant a bastion on the corner open to its trainees once a week, an inflexible, monolithic program, an isolated ecclesiastical island, a visible body moving collectively into troubled areas, the Church has been misinterpreted. There is a vast difference between organization and spirit, building and ministry, membership and mission, institution and charisma.

If by Church, however, is meant the people of God in concerned tension, repentance, pilgrimage, then the Church has never been more faithful. Contrary to criticism, professing Christians are increasingly more involved, concerned for the man "farthest down," more sensitive to inequities, less dedicated to denominations, more committed to Christ, more generous, compassionate, and determined to experience Christian community.

Due to the vision of the Area Council of Churches, Des Moines, Iowa, a four-million-dollar housing facility is in operation. Modest and low rents serve a genuine need. This and similar projects, initiated by churches in America and largely funded by the government, are indications of the public's belief in community-oriented services.

Consider the philanthropists, professional men and women, teachers, devoted Christians in America's cities quietly and effectively bearing witness through their work. Refined and growing person-to-person relationships will eventually nullify accusations, resentments, and violence. Understanding and love are busy building bridges of brotherhood. That which will heal the city, improve her image, increase her integrity, expand her stewardship, will be your demeanor and discipleship. Urban enrichment must take place as within a family; the strong must bear the burdens of the weak; the faithful must love the delinquent.

History asserts that man loves darkness over light. No amount of artificial lighting will increase his insights and farsights. There must be internal renewal before there can be external transformation. What if the occupants of your city really comprehended and had the courage to implement Jesus' declaration: "I am the light of the world; he who follows me will not walk in darkness, but will have the light of life" (John 8:12, RSV)?

There will always be a place in the city for people who recognize themselves as servants of Christ and who accept the challenge not only to remove man from the ghetto but the ghetto from man.

In a day of megalopolises, miasmas, conglomerates, confrontations, and group righteousness, God's candles must be kept burning with increasing brilliance. He needs more congregations with the stamina and faith of ancient Smyrna and Philadelphia.

During the 1960 presidential campaign, John Kennedy concluded a moving speech with the story of a judge in Hartford, Connecticut, who was presiding in court one morning in the middle seventeenth century when an eclipse of the sun occurred. The courtroom began to panic. Whereupon the judge rapped for order and said: "If this be the end of the world, let us at least be found doing our duty. Bring in the candles!"

NOTES

CHAPTER 2

1. Georgia Harkness, *Stability amid Change* (Nashville: Abingdon, 1969), p. 34. Used by permission.

2. Paul Tournier, *Are You Nobody?* (Richmond, Virginia: John Knox Press, 1967), p. 20. Used by permission.

CHAPTER 3

1. Robert A. Raines, *The Secular Congregation* (New York: Harper & Row, 1968), p. 24. Used by permission.

CHAPTER 5

1. From *Fire in Coventry* by Stephen Verney (London: Hodder & Stoughton) Copyright © 1964 by Stephen E. Verney.

CHAPTER 7

1. Jerome Ellison, *Report to the Creator* (New York: Harper & Bros., 1955), pp. 201, 205. Used by permission.